Beatrix Potter
99 Cliparts Book Part 4

15_Cliparts_Ginger.png

by
Elizabeth M. Potter

Content	Page

99 Cliparts

Bibliografische Information der Deutschen Nationalbibliothek:
Die Deutsche Nationalbibliothek verzeichnet diese Publikation in der Deutschen Nationalbibliografie; detaillierte bibliografische
Daten sind im Internet über http://dnb.dnb.de abrufbar.

© 2018 Elizabeth M. Potter 1. Auflage
Covergrafik, Texte und Bilder: © 2018 Elizabeth M. Potter

Herstellung und Verlag: BoD – Books on Demand, Norderstedt

ISBN: 9783752867107

The Tale of Jemima Puddle-Duck

1_Cliparts_Jemima.png

2_Cliparts_Jemima.png

3_Cliparts_Jemima.png

4_Cliparts_Jemima.png

5_Cliparts_Jemima.png

6_Cliparts_Jemima.png

7_Cliparts_Jemima.png

8_Cliparts_Jemima.png

9_Cliparts_Jemima.png

10_Cliparts_Jemima.png

11_Cliparts_Jemima.png

12_Cliparts_Jemima.png

13_Cliparts_Jemima.png

14_Cliparts_Jemima.png

15_Cliparts_Jemima.png

16_Cliparts_Jemima.png

17_Cliparts_Jemima.png

The Tale of Ginger and Pickles

1_Cliparts_Ginger.png

2_Cliparts_Ginger.png

3_Cliparts_Ginger.png

4_Cliparts_Ginger.png

5_Cliparts_Ginger.png

6_Cliparts_Ginger.png

7_Cliparts_TGinger.png

8_Cliparts_Ginger.png

9_Cliparts_Ginger.png

10_Cliparts_Ginger.png

11_Cliparts_Ginger.png

12_Cliparts_Ginger.png

13_Cliparts_Ginger.png

14_Cliparts_Ginger.png

15_Cliparts_Ginger.png

The Tale of Timmy Tiptoes

1_Cliparts_Timmy_Tiptoes.png

2_Cliparts_Timmy_Tiptoes.png

3_Cliparts_Timmy_Tiptoes.png

4_Cliparts_Timmy_Tiptoes.png

5_Cliparts_Timmy_Tiptoes.png

6_Cliparts_Timmy_Tiptoes.png

7_Cliparts_Timmy_Tiptoes.png

8_Cliparts_Timmy_Tiptoes.png

9_Cliparts_Timmy_Tiptoes.png

10_Cliparts_Timmy_Tiptoes.png

11_Cliparts_Timmy_Tiptoes.png

12_Cliparts_Timmy_Tiptoes.png

13_Cliparts_Timmy_Tiptoes.png

14_Cliparts_Timmy_Tiptoes.png

15_Cliparts_Timmy_Tiptoes.png

16_Cliparts_Timmy_Tiptoes.png

17_Cliparts_Timmy_Tiptoes.png

18_Cliparts_Timmy_Tiptoes.png

19_Cliparts_Timmy_Tiptoes.png

The Tale of Pigling Bland

1_Cliparts_Pigling.png

2_Cliparts_Pigling.png

3_Cliparts_Pigling.png

4_Cliparts_Pigling.png

5_Cliparts_Pigling.png

6_Cliparts_Pigling.png

7_Cliparts_Pigling.png

8_Cliparts_Pigling.png

9_Cliparts_Pigling.png

10_Cliparts_Pigling.png

11_Cliparts_Pigling.png

12_Cliparts_Pigling.png

13_Cliparts_Pigling.png

14_Cliparts_Pigling.png

15_Cliparts_Pigling.png

16_Cliparts_Pigling.png

17_Cliparts_Pigling .png

18_Cliparts_Pigling .png

19_Cliparts_Pigling .png

20_Cliparts_Pigling.png

The Tale of Little Pig Robinson

1_Cliparts_Robinson.png

2_Cliparts_Robinson.png

3_Cliparts_Robinson.png

4_Cliparts_Robinson.png

5_Cliparts_Robinson.png

6_Cliparts_Robinson.png

7_Cliparts_Robinson.png

8_Cliparts_Robinson.png

9_Cliparts_Robinson.png

10_Cliparts_Robinson.png

11_Cliparts_Robinson.png

12_Cliparts_Robinson.png

13_Cliparts_Robinson.png

14_Cliparts_Robinson.png

15_Cliparts_Robinson.png

2nd Part of link: **AAArpV4k3fWZdEphA5knaCuAa?dl=0**

Apple Dapply's Nursery Rhymes

1_Cliparts_Appley.png

2_Cliparts_Appley.png

3_Cliparts_Appley.png

4_Cliparts_Appley.png

5_Cliparts_Appley.png

6_Cliparts_Appley.png

7_Cliparts_Appley.png

8_Cliparts_Appley.png

9_Cliparts_Appley.png

10_Cliparts_Appley.png

11_Cliparts_Appley.png

Hase.png

Hase_auf Fahrrad.png

Hase_trinkt_Tee.png

Peter_Hase_Postbote.png

Instructions for downloading the Cliparts

Before you are reading the instructions to download/using the cliparts, please read the following handling instructions for the correct usage of the cliparts.

Handling instruction for the usage of the cliparts

The cliparts were created by Elizabeth M. Potter. Therefore please take into account the following before starting the download:

You can use the cliparts for any of your private enterprises, projects, presentations, invitations or the like.
But it is not allowed to use them for commercial purpurses.
If you intend to use them for commercial purpurses, please ask for written approval by Elizabeth M. Potter in advance (elizabeth.potter@t-online.de).
In that case, publishing, republishing or reproductions of the cliparts, especially of the download link, via any kind of service, Internet or graphic service wether as a book, electronically, or via other not listed above media or other means, without prior approval by Elizabeth M. Potter is strongly prohibited.

- -

Clipart download instructions

The cliparts are in a directory of dropbox Service. It is a simple access by typing in the download link into your internet browser. The access is possible via PC, smartphone or tablet. The clipart files are presented in png-format.
For security reasons the link is divided into two parts. For gaining the complete link, both parts have to be typed into the address field of the browser one after another without spaces in between.

1st Part of link: **https://www.dropbox.com/sh/5lqizjja3wdx6f4/**
2nd Part of link: you will find on page 20 of this book

Further books of Elizabeth M. Potter

NOTEBOOKS
The Peter Rabbit Notebook
PAINTING BOOKS
Beatrix Potter Painting Book Part 1 (Peter Rabbit)
Beatrix Potter Painting Book Part 2 (Peter Rabbit)
Beatrix Potter Painting Book Part 3 (Peter Rabbit)
Beatrix Potter Painting Book Part 4 (Peter Rabbit)
Beatrix Potter Painting Book Part 5 (Peter Rabbit)
Beatrix Potter Painting Book Part 6 (Peter Rabbit)
Beatrix Potter Painting Book Part 7 (Peter Rabbit)
Beatrix Potter Painting Book Part 8 (Peter Rabbit)
Beatrix Potter Painting Book Part 9 (Peter Rabbit)
Beatrix Potter Painting Book Part 10 (Peter Rabbit)
Peter Rabbit Painting Book
CLIPART BOOKS
Beatrix Potter 99 Cliparts Book Part 1 (Peter Rabbit)
Beatrix Potter 99 Cliparts Book Part 2 (Peter Rabbit)
Beatrix Potter 99 Cliparts Book Part 3 (Peter Rabbit)
Beatrix Potter 99 Cliparts Book Part 4 (Peter Rabbit)
PASSWORD BOOKS
The Peter Rabbit Passwortbook